READING CHAMPION

Sandy Cove
Rescue

by Sue Graves and Noémie Gionet Landry

W

Chapter 1

Jess and Spencer were best friends. They went to Sandy Cove School, which was by the sea. Year 4 had been learning about the local environment. Jess and Spencer really enjoyed it. They liked learning about the beach and the rock pools, and finding out about the wildlife that lived in them.

our environment

Dolphin
Dolphins are very smart!

OUR FISH

SEALS
Seals can hold their breath for 2 hours under water

ALGAE
Many types. The most common is KELP

Starfish
Have 5 arm. Arms can grow back!

One day, a visitor came to the school.

"This is Frankie," said their teacher, Mr Sharma.

"She is a helper at the Sandy Cove Animal

Rescue Centre."

Frankie told the children all about her job.

"It is really interesting," she said, "but there are problems, too. Lots of people visit our beach every day. Some people are thoughtful and put their litter into the bins. Others even take their litter home with them. But some just drop litter everywhere."

5

Then Frankie showed them pictures of the beach.

It was covered with old cans and bits of plastic.

"Litter pollutes the beach and the sea,"

she explained. "A polluted environment harms

our wildlife."

"Why don't you put up posters telling people not to drop litter?" Jess asked.

"We have," replied Frankie. "But some people don't take any notice. So we have to check the beach for litter regularly."

At the end of the lesson, Frankie had some news to share. She said that there was going to be a big beach clean on Saturday. She asked if anyone could help.

Jess and Spencer quickly put up their hands.

Lots of other hands shot up too!

"Excellent!" said Frankie. "Come to Sandy Cove beach at 9 o'clock sharp. I'll be there with your teachers to show you what to do. You will work together in pairs to help clean up the beach."

Chapter 2

Jess and Spencer got to the beach early
on Saturday morning. Frankie gave them each
a litter-picker and a large bin bag.
"You must keep together," she said. "Do not
pick up the litter with your hands. Make sure
you use the litter-pickers."

Jess tried to nip Spencer with her litter-picker.

"Please be sensible," warned Mr Sharma,

looking at Jess. "And take care on the rocks.

They are slippery and I don't want any accidents."

"Yes, Mr Sharma," said the children.

Jess and Spencer walked to the far end
of the beach. They got to work quickly.
It wasn't long before their bin bags were full.
"All this rubbish!" said Jess, peering into her bag.
"Look, I've found a flip-flop and a broken bucket.
Look at all these empty crisp packets, too."

Spencer picked up an old sun hat.

"Someone left this on the beach." He put the hat

on his head. "How do I look?" he asked.

"Really silly," laughed Jess.

The children worked on for a while longer,
but the sun was getting hotter and hotter.
"Let's have a rest and a drink of water,"
said Spencer.

Jess pointed to some big rocks where it was
shady. "We could sit there," she said.
"It will be cooler."

The children sat down and drank some water.

Suddenly they heard a strange scraping noise.

It was coming from behind the rocks.

"What's that?" asked Jess.

"I don't know," said Spencer. "Perhaps it's pirates!"

"Or a huge sea monster," said Jess.

The noise got louder and louder.

"Check it out, Jess," said Spencer.

He gave her a little push.

"No, *you* check it out," said Jess.

"Let's both go," said Spencer. "But you go first,"

he added nervously, looking at the rocks.

Jess and Spencer climbed carefully up on the slippery rocks. They looked through a gap. There, on the beach, was a seal pup lying on a rock. The seal had an old plastic can holder around its neck. It was trying hard to free itself.

Jess and Spencer ducked back down

so they did not frighten the seal pup.

"I wish people didn't drop litter," muttered Jess

crossly. "Look at the harm it does."

"What can we do?" asked Spencer. He looked

worried. "The pup needs to be freed quickly."

"But what if the pup's mum is still around?" said

Jess. "If she sees us, she won't come back to feed

it any more."

Jess wasn't sure how to help the seal.

"Go and get Frankie," she told Spencer.

"She'll know what to do. I'll stay and keep watch
to see if the pup's mum comes back."

"That's a great idea. I'll be back as soon as I can,"
promised Spencer. He ran off.

The sun rose higher in the sky. The pup was getting
hot and tired. Jess got more and more worried,
and there was no sign of the seal pup's mother.

"Help is on its way," she whispered to the seal pup.

"It won't be long now."

Chapter 3

After what seemed like an hour, Frankie appeared with Spencer and Mr Sharma.

"Well done for keeping back," Frankie told Jess. "Seal pups can give a nasty bite. And you might have scared away his mother, although this pup looks old enough to have left his mother by now."

"I haven't seen any other seals come near the beach," said Jess.

Frankie went to examine the young animal.

"This is serious," she said. "He has a deep cut

on one side of his neck. We'll need to take him

to the rescue centre. He can't go back

into the sea until the wound has healed."

Frankie and Mr Sharma wrapped the seal

in a blanket and gently carried him off the beach.

Jess and Spencer were worried.

"Will he be okay?" asked Spencer.

"Don't worry, you two," said Frankie. She smiled

at them. "The seal will be safe at the centre."

Chapter 4

Two weeks later, Mr Sharma came over

to Jess and Spencer as they were working.

He told them that Frankie was on the phone

and she wanted to talk to them.

They hurried to the office.

"Is the seal pup okay?" asked Spencer.

"Yes," said Frankie. "The pup's wound has healed

well, and he's shown us that he is a good swimmer

and can look after himself. So would you two like

to help me return him to the sea?"

"Yes!" shouted Spencer.

"You bet!" said Jess. "That would be amazing."

After school, the children raced down to meet
Frankie at the beach. The seal pup was in a cage
on the sand.

"He looks so much better," said Jess.

"Right," said Frankie. "It's time to let this little one
go back to the sea. Undo the cage door, you two.
Stay nice and quiet. We don't want to frighten him."

Jess and Spencer opened the door and stood still.

The seal poked his nose out of the door and sniffed the air. He lifted his head towards the sea and slid towards the water.

Then, with a loud splash, the pup plunged under the waves and swam strongly out to sea.

"The seal's made it!" said Spencer, happily.

Jess agreed. "He'll be safe now," she said.

Things to think about

1. Have you learned about the local environment at your school?
2. Why do you think some people leave litter behind?
3. Do you think we should help clean up this litter, even if it is not our mess?
4. Do you think Jess and Spencer are sensible when they pick up litter? Are they sensible after they see the seal?
5. Why is Frankie pleased they did not approach the seal?

Write it yourself

One of the themes in this story is caring for the environment. Now try to write your own story with a similar theme.

Plan your story before you begin to write it.

Start off with a story map:

• a beginning to introduce the characters and where and when your story is set (the setting);

• a problem which the main characters will need to fix in the story;

• an ending where the problems are resolved.

Get writing! Try to create interesting characters, not just by telling your reader what they are like, but showing this through their actions. For example, Jess and Spencer have fun, but they are sensible when they need to be.

Notes for parents and carers

Independent reading

The aim of independent reading is to read this book with ease. This series is designed to provide an opportunity for your child to read for pleasure and enjoyment. These notes are written for you to help your child make the most of this book.

About the book

This story is about the rescue of a wounded seal pup who has become caught in a plastic drink holder. He is discovered by two children who are on a beach clean. Luckily, they know enough about seal welfare to know how to fetch help, and the seal can be reintroduced to the wild after a stay at the rescue centre.

Before reading

Ask your child why they have selected this book. Look at the title and blurb together. What do they think it will be about? Do they think they will like it?

During reading

Encourage your child to read independently. If they get stuck on a longer word, remind them that they can find syllable chunks that can be sounded out from left to right. They can also read on in the sentence and think about what would make sense.

After reading

Support comprehension by talking about the story. What happened?
Then help your child think about the messages in the book that go beyond the story, using the questions on the page opposite. Give your child a chance to respond to the story, asking:
Did you enjoy the story and why? Who was your favourite character?
What was your favourite part? What did you expect to happen at the end?

Franklin Watts
First published in Great Britain in 2018
by The Watts Publishing Group

Series Editors: Jackie Hamley and Melanie Palmer
Series Advisors: Dr Sue Bodman and Glen Franklin
Series Designer: Peter Scoulding

A CIP catalogue record for this book is
available from the British Library.

ISBN 978 1 4451 6319 2 (hbk)
ISBN 978 1 4451 6320 8 (pbk)
ISBN 978 1 4451 6318 5 (library ebook)

Printed in China

Franklin Watts
An imprint of
Hachette Children's Group
Part of The Watts Publishing Group
Carmelite House
50 Victoria Embankment
London EC4Y 0DZ

An Hachette UK Company
www.hachette.co.uk

www.franklinwatts.co.uk

FSC
www.fsc.org
MIX
Paper from
responsible sources
FSC® C104740